P9-CRS-074

LANGUAGE SKILLS FOR THE

YOUNG CHILD

A TEACHER'S GUIDE OF LANGUAGE

SKILLS FOR THE PRESCHOOL

AND PRIMARY GRADES

By Lynn Simonds

Printed in 1975

R AND E RESEARCH ASSOCIATES
4843 Mission Street, San Francisco 94112
18581 McFarland Avenue, Saratoga, California 95070

Publishers and Distributors of Ethnic Studies
Editor: Adam S. Eterovich
Publisher: Robert D. Reed

Library of Congress Card Catalog Number

74-20273

ISBN

0-88247-303-4

FOREWORD

As a kindergarten teacher with a very practical knowledge of young children, Lynn Simonds has gathered together some of her effective techniques for developing children's language. From her wide range of personal experiences she shares with teachers in this publication her ideas and activities which enable children to develop within themselves not only language but also feelings of success.

The child who says, "I can do it myself" is a child who can find school a rewarding experience. Mrs. Simonds invites teachers to include in their classroom practices techniques which will enable each child to develop positive feelings of self.

To you readers I suggest a careful perusal of the following pages and a reminder to use the Bibliography for finding extensions of her ideas.

Happy Reading!

Margaret Smart, Ph. D.
Associate Professor of Early Childhood Education
University of Southern California

TABLE OF CONTENTS

INTRODUCTION

A balanced program with clearly defined goals is of crucial importance for young children. The communication skills form the basis for achievement in other areas and are interwoven with personal development and self-concept. As learning is highly personal, the children should feel that their individual contributions are important in their classroom and to their teacher. Through language activities, they set the standards, take part in decisions involving routines, decide ways to keep their room attractive and undertake the responsibility for looking after materials and classroom pets. Effective teachers know that language abilities are strengthened daily by the children being exposed to a wide variety of activities which can be used to teach all aspects of the language arts in relation to curriculum content.

Working on language development involves four specific areas:

1. Phonology--increased ability to use sounds

2. Semantics--increased ability to use words, meanings, and concepts of the language

3. Syntax--increased ability to use the structure of language

4. Morphology--increased ability to use grammatical markers in the language. This includes ing, ed, plural s, possessive s. Correct, accurate knowledge of tense usage is included in morphological development.

Teachers should be aware of these areas and sensitive to inherent difficulties in each.

Recent studies have shown that there is a high correlation between listening and speaking, and between speaking and writing. The teacher should therefore use every method at her disposal to help children to speak and listen more effectively. Ways in which this may be accomplished are suggested in this book. Generally speaking, the suggestions herein are intended for use by teachers of preschool and kindergarten children but many can be adapted for use by teachers of the primary grades.

CHAPTER I

USING LANGUAGE TO BUILD SELF-CONCEPT

In any discussion referring
to learning, the matter of self-concept
is important. The real worth of any
program for young children lies not
only in content but in the way it
contributes to each child's sense of
worth. A teacher can make or break
a child's self-image which is directly
related to his language development.

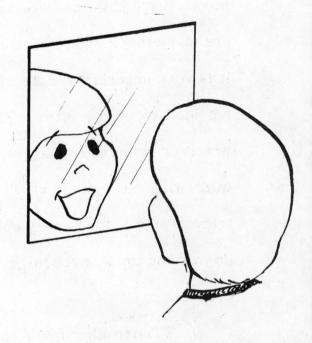

Only when a child has confidence in himself is he ready to learn.
Feelings of worthlessness are sometimes so ingrained that it is difficult
to overcome them. Children who grow up in a disorganized and chaotic
environment are sometimes difficult to reach. Current learning theory
indicates that when children's basic needs are not satisfied, they do not
learn to trust adults and therefore they do not cooperate with them. The
teacher needs to be very sure that the children feel secure in the
knowledge that she likes them and has a great deal of faith in them. A
consistent environment is desirable for the children's growth. Individual

activities have to be clearly planned and demonstrated. Not all children come from homes where they are used to initiating projects; it should not be assumed that they will be able to "find a job." The teacher, therefore, has to help children to use their activity time in acceptable ways. Some children have so little self-direction, however, that there are many times when a teacher has to deal with unacceptable behavior. It is very important for the child's self-concept that the teacher should not adopt a punitive attitude and that the child understands the reason for whatever action is necessary. Young children have had little experience in relating cause to effect. Thus, a child who repeatedly crashes his tricycle into another, may not understand the necessity for slowing down some time before he needs to stop; failure to do this causes the crash.

The teacher needs to differentiate between the child and his behavior and instead of making a value judgment, give the child an "out," thus showing her faith in him. The way in which verbal directions are given makes all the difference to the outcome. The child with problem tendencies is more likely than another to react by refusing to comply. Simple, constructive, directive, unhurried, and approving verbal directions are usually more effective with all children than those which contain negative and reproving elements. The teacher should make every effort to establish rapport with each child at times other than when he is demanding attention and to channel behavior as much as possible within the program framework; not here but there, not now but later, not that but this. Children come to school from families with widely differing value systems and what is normal behavior at home may be unacceptable in a classroom situation. Care should be taken, therefore, not to give the child the impression that certain behavior is wrong or bad, but merely inappropriate. He has to learn, however, that what is appropriate in one place may be inappropriate in another but this takes a great deal of time, patience, and effort on the part of the teacher. The less she imposes her own values upon the situation, the better her understanding of the child and the better the chances of his developing a healthy self-concept. When children have difficulty with materials or in working with others, they should be encouraged to solve their problems constructively. Children who forget safety standards can be asked to state the rule and the reason for it before using the materials. If the teacher pleasantly voices her positive expectations and reinforces acceptable behavior as soon as it occurs, most types of discipline problems can be avoided. If misbehavior persists, however, no time should be lost in psychological referral. The majority of children are evaluated only after damaging periods of scholastic failure.

Children can be helped to understand their own and others' strengths and weaknesses by talking about them. Mary M. Green's book, "Is It Hard? Is It Easy?" is a good springboard for this type of discussion.

If the teacher does something for a child that he is able to do for himself, she is implying that she can do it better. If a child has not yet learned to tie his shoe, asking another child to do it motivates the one to learn and reinforces the self-concept of the helper. Helping children to become responsible human beings is best done in a spirit of love, respect, confidence, and trust. They must be set free to discover their own worth. They can be encouraged to make thoughtful decisions, to talk and think about their feelings and to accept their limitations.

The teacher should remember to call on each child by name when she is talking with him. The children's names should be prominently displayed; on charts, on art work, and wherever else is appropriate. It is helpful for the children to see their names on the top left corner of any art work and written in manuscript, as this will be the way it will be done all through school.

A camera should be an indispensable item for the teacher. Photographs can be used in many ways. Each photograph can be slipped into a library book pocket and enough cut from the front side of the pocket to frame the picture. The child's name can be printed on the pocket, which could also be decorated by the child. These pictures can then be used to identify art work, in a file or on bulletin boards. A discussion about standards pertaining to riding as a passenger can be highlighted by a bulletin board bus, or car using photographs of the children as passengers. Another bulletin board idea is to depict the Old Woman Who Lived in a Shoe. Photographs of the children who can

4

tie bows can be taped behind cut-out windows in a large construction paper shoe with real laces. Pictures thus displayed often motivate children to learn a new skill. Beginning understandings in mathematics can be stimulated by photographs of the children using ropes and balls to find out how many times they can bounce, or jump the rope. This information can be dictated by the children and written underneath photographs mounted on colored construction paper and made into a book for the reading corner.

Photographs can also be used on special charts for birthdays, or hung as decorations from a Christmas tree. They can be placed so that the children's faces appear to be looking out of windows of the houses they have made as the result of learning their addresses. Photographs can be sent home as part of a Mother's Day gift or mounted in a class album. They can be used on a map showing where children were born or have visited. Even a group school photograph can be used in imaginative ways. Each idea can be used in some type of language activity. Children who are hesitant to talk can often recall the details of a situation by looking at their photograph; what they were doing and wearing and who else was there. Photographs should not be limited to those of the children. Activities such as block building, which necessitates the putting away of materials, can be preserved on film for the children to keep.

Not all children know their birthdays and sometimes they go by

at home without mention. Discarded school library books can sometimes be found which only need new covers which can be decorated with
cut-outs from old greeting cards and sent home as gifts. Children enjoy
a special hat or headband made out of tag in the form of a crown or
candles which they can color and take home. A special birthday chart
can be made showing a picture of a cake; a slit can be cut in the chart
for the insertion of a birthday napkin for snack time; the child's
photograph can be slipped into a pocket at the bottom of the chart on
which is written Happy Birthday. The book, or balloon, and the headband
can then be slipped into the pocket so that all is ready when the child
arrives. Appropriate art materials can be available for those children
who would like to make a birthday card. The birthday child is allowed
to choose his favorite story and a friend to sit by. The other children
can form a circle making a "cake" while the birthday child chooses four,
five, or six of his friends to be "candles." They stand in the center,
each with palms together over their heads to represent wicks. The
birthday child "lights" and "blows out" his candles after everyone has
sung a birthday song. Each "candle" puts his hands down after he has
been "blown out." A mimeographed birthday certificate can be
completed by the teacher and given to the child for him to paste on a
greeting card picture of his choice.

Accessories used to promote children's language skills should
include dolls, books, and pictures depicting a variety of ethnic groups.

Full length and small mirrors, large bars of soap, and jars of hand cream for children to use are relatively inexpensive and well worth their cost in the efforts children will make to be clean and well-groomed.

It is important for the teacher to know each child's status in the group. Many singing games depend on one child choosing another and over a period of time, the teacher can note which children are not chosen. Mimeographed lists of names are useful in many ways and can be used quickly by the teacher when the children are choosing each other for various activities. Occasionally, it escapes the teacher's notice that there is a child with whom none of the others choose to play over a long period. A more direct method of finding out how children feel about each other is through the aid of a sociogram. Each child is asked separately, "Who do you like best in school?" Children's names are written randomly on a page and arrows are drawn from each child's name to his choice. Names having no arrows pointing to them are therefore those of children whom no one has mentioned and they may need help in relating to others. It should be remembered, however, that children's relationships are in constant flux and too much signifi- cance should probably not be inferred from such methods. They can, on occasion, however, be helpful, and teachers are often surprised at how little their own assumptions and children's choices coincide. Through skillful maneuvering, teachers can sometimes bring together children who have like interests and widen the circle of those who are too heavily dependent on each other. When children are not included in the play of others, they can be helped to understand that if they contribute something, they are more likely to be accepted. This contribution can be anything from food for the animals to an offer to help pull the wagon or deliver the mail.

Every effort should be made to personalize the learning process. Substituting an inattentive child's name for the one in the story often helps. Spontaneous singing is an effective attention-getter. All the ways in which the children contribute to ideas used in the program help to enhance self-concept. Every effort should be made to see that as many children as possible participate in many ways in <u>every</u> learning situation. The skilful teacher knows that reinforcing acceptable behavior is far more effective than commenting upon unacceptable behavior. Praise should be given for specific learnings, thus, "John is learning how to write his name and I'm so proud of him," rather than, "John is getting to be such a big boy."

The teacher's role is vital in the development of the young child's self-concept. She has a strong responsibility to provide a happy, flexible environment in which the child will feel free to learn. She knows and recognizes each as a unique individual and encourages him to express himself in as many ways as possible. She protects children from unwise pressures. She sets reasonable limits in an atmosphere which is conducive to spontaneous, unselfconscious speech. She encourages self-selection of activities for the child to satisfy his personal needs and interests, thus allowing him to reveal his feelings and concerns. She shows confidence in each child's ability to succeed and gives praise for each contribution.

Evaluating Self-concept

It is very difficult for teachers to ascertain a young child's self-concept. The following questions may be helpful to the teacher in understanding children's feelings and in suggesting ways in which the child can be helped.

Does the child appear to be socially adequate?

(accepted by other children; sometimes accepted; excluded from other children's play)

Is the child able to compete physically with the other children?

(able to do what they do; some of what they do; little of what they do)

Is the child able to compete intellectually with other children?

(is able to but dominates them; is able to but is so shy they are unaware of the fact . . .)

Is the child physically unattractive?

(handicapped, has some deformity, unclean, shabbily dressed)

Does the child appear to be apprehensive of new activities?

(feels adequate to face whatever comes, feels fearful of attempting anything unknown)

Does the child depend a great deal on adult attention?

>(by asking for help; by clinging; by relying on suggestions for activities . . .)

How does the child react to exclusion or aggression?

>(by withdrawing; by verbal retaliation; by physical attack; by fantasy; by creative activity; by tears . . .)

Does the child seem to feel secure in his parent relationships and in his relationships with teachers?

>(parental over-protection; parental under-protection . . .)

What assets are available to solve his problem?

>(loving family; special talents; positive characteristics)

What liabilities are making it difficult for him to accomplish his developmental tasks?

>(overt aggression; extreme shyness; unattractive appearance, immature behavior . . .)

What effect does he seem to produce upon his peers?

>(dislike; aggression; apathy . . .)

Have his former relationships been happy?

>(Sunday school group; preschool . . .)

Are there any records available?

>(social agencies, preschool, medical . . .)

How good are his sibling relationships?

When does he appear to be happiest?

With whom does he appear to be happiest?

CHAPTER II

SETTING THE STAGE FOR LANGUAGE EXPERIENCES

Speaking

When children speak, they
have opportunity to learn to organize
their thoughts and express them in
words suitable for conveying their
meaning to others. It is the teacher's
responsibility to help children to speak
clearly and audibly; to express ideas
in whole thought units; to increase
vocabulary; to participate in discussions
by contributing relevant information and by waiting for a turn to talk;
to recognize and express both positive and negative feelings in self and
others; to ask questions; to expand and clarify information; and to
solve problems verbally. There are many ways of working towards
these goals; some are listed hereunder.

Conversation.

Group discussion.

Expressing feelings and ideas.

Seeking and sharing information.

Formulating questions and answers.

Giving and following directions.

Rhyming.

Conversation

Adequate opportunities for language development through
conversation will not occur without planning. Language as a means of
communication must be increasingly used by the children before they
are able to achieve any degree of mastery over it. Language flourishes
in a classroom where children participate with enthusiasm in many
activities. First-hand observation and experiences act as a stimulant
to language growth. Conversation can be encouraged through the use of
puppets. The shy child tends to lose his apprehension when he speaks
for a puppet. Stick puppets can sometimes be made using cut-outs
from the children's easel paintings or drawings which have been
mounted on tag. Children enjoy making puppet heads on tag cut-outs
from scraps of collage materials such as foil, macaroni, ribbon,
sequins, discarded jewelry, and yarn. Tongue depressors can be
stapled on as holders. These characters can be named by the children
and can converse about suggested incidents or talk spontaneously.

12

Particularly shy children often begin using puppets by making them dance to music. A piece of material with hooks at each end to be attached to each side of a doorway or alcove makes an easy screen.

Children enjoy talking on the telephones in the housekeeping area. Obsolete telephones are sometimes obtainable from the telephone company. Using a 6-volt battery, it is possible to connect them so that children can actually hear each other's voices. This activity can be formal or unstructured. Some children have no telephone at home and will need help in deciding upon possible reasons for a phone call.

Snack time is an educational experience as well as being conducive to conversation. The children talk about things which are important to them within a social framework. With encouragement from the teacher they learn the courtesies of "please," "thank you," and "may I have?"

The children should be expected to verbalize their choice of activity and not merely be asked what they might like to do. "Are you going to work with the clay? Tell me." If some are unable to do this, the teacher should verbalize for them until they can. Saying, "I see you decided to work with a puzzle," helps children to think in terms of their own activities and gives a label to those materials they do not always know how to name.

Associative thinking should be encouraged by the teacher for its own value and for the opportunity it gives children to verbalize. Saying,

"Do you need a sweater before you go outside?" usually has the effect

of the child merely getting it, but saying "What do you need before you

go outside?" serves a double purpose. Children should be encouraged

to use whatever dialect they speak. They must orally develop and

amplify sentences until they are using the full range of their linguistic

potential.

Group discussion

Discussion is an activity which should hold a prominent place

in the classroom. Children learn to analyze and clarify ideas, to add

to their vocabulary, to practice oral language skills, and to exercise

their imagination. On these occasions, two rules must be observed;

only one person speaks at a time and there is no right or wrong answer.

The following topics are suggested:

Where would you go in an airplane?
What if you woke up and were only as big as a finger?
What would you like to do for a day?
What would we do if there were no money?
Why is the sky?
What kind of monster would you like to be?
What if you changed from a boy to a girl?
Suppose you had three arms, legs . . .
If someone gave you a dollar, what would you do with it?
Suppose you were the only person in the whole world?
What have you done to help somebody?
Suppose you lost your voice?
Do you have an imaginary playmate?

During these sessions, the teacher's role should be one of

mediator and interpreter. Misconceptions should be discussed on

another occasion. Ten minutes discussion is usually enough for most young children although this period can be extended as interest span lengthens. Children should sit in a circle.

Field trips offer many opportunities for language growth, among them opportunities for discussion. Although it is not always possible for classes to have frequent bus trips, much learning can result from walks in the neighborhood. The discussion before children leave includes the standards to be observed on the walk, and what to look out for. There should always be an aim: to collect rocks or leaves, to look for different types of buildings, or shapes; to develop new concepts; to buy ingredients for a cooking experience or any number of others. Before going on a listening walk, the children can try to think of what sounds they might hear. These should be listed for later discussion. The same procedure should be followed for other kinds of walks. Children could be grouped to look for specific colors, each accompanying adult helping children to record what they observed, for later sharing. Did the children looking for red things find more than the children who looked for blue? Children can record their observations by marking with a crayon on an acetate-covered cardboard "pocket," strung with yarn and worn around their necks. A piece of white paper can be slipped between the cardboard and the acetate for easier visibility and the crayon markings can be erased later. A small piece of colored paper can be inserted into the "pocket" or children could mark their board with the color crayon for which they are looking. The teacher will find these boards very useful as they can also be used when children are looking for specific letters or numerals on their walks. They can be worn in the housekeeping corner. "I am mother," or in the classroom restaurant, "I am the waitress." They can be used to act out stories. "I am the giant."

A weekly walk could be a feature of the program and could be followed by a story dictated by the children or a small group of children with a photograph to illustrate it. Some teachers make a class book in this way which the children discuss throughout the year; it helps remind them of what they have learned.

Expressing feelings and ideas

Children can be very creative and their ideas can be elicited in many ways and in many areas of the language arts program. Sensory experiences particularly lend themselves to self-expression in vivid imagery and vocabulary. Children can be encouraged to talk about their feelings after hearing music or poetry. They can interpret pictures in their own way, expressing their own ideas as to what happened before and after the incident portrayed. Old greeting cards are sometimes fun to use. Libraries often throw away book jackets showing interesting pictures. Those which are open to a variety of interpretations and which evoke an emotional response help children to express their feelings. Children in a small group can each be given, or choose, a picture to study. The teacher then says something about each in turn.

The child who thinks the statement appropriate to his picture says why he thinks so. Children could make a set of paper bag masks each showing a feeling and wear them when they talk.

Accessories of many kinds can be used for self-expression. Puppets, dolls, and block accessories are essential items in the classroom and should reflect the ethnic backgrounds of the children.

Children are apt to express negative feelings physically. They need much help and much practice in verbalizing them. The teacher can help children to become more aware of them. "I think you're mad because Johnny pushed you. What could you have said to Johnny?" When two children are having a problem getting along, it can be helpful for them to sit down to decide what happened. The teacher expresses her faith in them being able to work it out. Although this is difficult for some children, it gives them opportunities to search for words before they can resume what they were doing. Usually this occupies them so completely, that the original problem is forgotten. They are also interested in getting back to whatever they were doing and reconciliation is almost inevitable. Problem solving is therefore raised to a verbal level. The teacher should be alert to the fact that new phraseology and vocabulary can always be introduced with new experiences and that immediate discussion of feelings following them result in translation into fresh and vivid words.

A tape recorder is sometimes invaluable in getting shy children

17

to talk. Ask them to tell about a picture which would have appeal to children, or about their favorite television show, toy, or person. Ask them about the funniest, happiest, scariest thing that happened to them. Accept one-word answers until the child is able to say more. Model larger structure:

> Question:"What's this?"
>
> Answer: "Apple"
>
> Teacher: "Yes, it is an apple." Keep structure very simple, responding to his correctness and amplifying his structure.

Tell him briefly the funniest thing that happened to you!

Make up a group story by looking at a group picture with much detail. One child says something about it and then the next contributes another sentence and so on. Ask children how they behave when they are sad, mad, and happy. Divide the children into three groups to represent those feelings. Make up a story which includes those elements. Every time the teacher says   those three words, the children in that group show how they behave by crying, stamping their feet, clapping their hands, jumping up and down, or whatever else they have suggested. An example of the story follows.

Mother said she would take Joe and Mary to the zoo. That made them very happy (H). Their little brother was too little to go and that made him sad (S). The next day mother had a toothache and had to go to the dentist so they couldn't go after all (S), but mother said they could go the next day if she was better (H). She <u>was</u> better, but it was raining and that made them mad (M), but they made cookies instead (H). But they made a mistake and used salt instead of sugar so they had to throw them away (M). The next day they woke up and Joe had a tummy ache (S). Mother made him take some medicine (M), but he soon felt better (H). On the way to the zoo they got a flat tire (M), but got it mended (H). At the zoo they saw a _____ which didn't like being in a cage (S). Joe teased it which made it mad (M). Keeper fed it (H). Finally mother said it was time to go home (M) and they had to say goodbye to the animals (S). Then little brother was happy to see them (H). For supper they had _____ (H), but Mary didn't like _____ and mother said she must eat a little (M). Then it was time for bed (M), but when they thought of their day at the zoo they were _____ (H).

Seeking and sharing information

Children need to understand that there are many ways of finding and communicating facts. By watching television they can find out about certain products or events. After being asked by the teacher to watch a certain commercial, some children will enjoy giving it on the class "television set." By referring to the teacher's file, they can find the shape of a truck for their block building; a certain book will include a picture of a tadpole for their easel painting. Children can learn to find adults who specialize, first at school, and then in the community. They can understand that photographs, films, and filmstrips are sources of information. By listening to a transistor radio, they can determine the kinds of things they can learn from it. Looking at paintings and portraits helps them to realize that artists can sometimes answer our questions. Examining bones and fossils teaches them another way of finding information. Children learn that their own senses and bodies can instruct. Tracks and fingerprints can be made and displayed. All these facts can be brought out in class and children should be given practice in using and sharing information.

The Show and Tell Time is an important part of many programs. Of recent years this practice seems to have fallen into disrepute. There is no denying the fact that getting up and speaking in front of a group is good preparation for later reading in front of a group. Many children, however, can bring nothing from home which would be of interest to the group and their peers have not developed the listening skills necessary for this practice to be successful. There are a number of ways to get around this problem. A teacher could keep a bell which children may ring during activity time if they wish to share something with the other children, thus only the interested listeners gather round. In some schools, sharing is the result of specific inquiry. The teacher asks the children to observe some particular object on the way home and come next day prepared to talk about it. Those who remember are eager to contribute this kind of information. Items within the class can be shared. The teacher can explore a new plant with a specific child, helping him name and describe it. Later, this child can share his knowledge with the class. In this way the teacher can prepare his success and structure his reinforcement.

Children enjoy sharing information about their work projects. Showing his easel painting or block building gives the child the verbal clues he needs for effective communication. Children learn to value everyone's contribution in this way.

Formulating questions and answers

Many children miss out on learning opportunities because of their failure to ask questions. If they don't understand, they are likely to pretend they do, or guess. Teaching children that they can ask questions when they need additional information is important. Play the game, "What Can He Do?" Ask a child to ask another a question such as "What can a kitten do?" The second child answers "A kitten can drink milk." This child then asks another "What can a baby do?" and so on.

Have a child say something about his toy or pet. Ask the others what they would like to know about it, and encourage them to question. The telephone game can be played using questions and answers. One child is chosen as the operator--most rooms have some sort of gadget board which can double as a switchboard. The caller is instructed to ask a question and the listener to answer it. Children can decide what questions are appropriate to ask the fire department, the supermarket, the doctor.

Before a visitor comes to the room, the children should be guided to formulate a list of questions regarding what they would like to know. After the visitor has gone, the answers to their questions can be discussed. Children never seem to tire of asking questions of the teacher if she encourages them. They love to hear about her children, her pets, her home. All questioning involves speaking in complete sentences which is valuable in itself. Questions asked by the teacher can be structured for children who are hesitant to talk. "Are you holding a blue shape or a red shape?" Through these kinds of questions, the teacher gives the language and the child chooses the response. As the children develop more fluency, the questions allow for a high level of response.

Another way of helping children learn to formulate questions is to place a collection of objects out which would be of interest to children and say, "I'm thinking of one of those things. You can ask me questions and find out which one and I can only answer yes, or no."

Dr. Margaret Smart uses a collection of gloves for this purpose, including those used for gardening, evening wear, and barbequeing. They can also be used for making pairs and for classifying.

With each new encountered item in the classroom, go through the five w's: what, who, where, when, and why. Children learn structure by modeling it and need the model in consistent, repetitive fashion.

Giving and following directions

There are many games children can play which help to develop their ability to give and follow directions. Pieces of paper cut into geometric shapes or in different colors, depending on current learning, can be put in a box. On each shape is written a direction which is read to the child. For example: Go to the bookshelf, take a book, and sit down. Directions of increasing complexity can be given as the children are ready. "Walk to the bookshelf, take a small book, and sit down." When the child performs correctly, he gives the same direction to the adult. This gives the teacher some insight as to his ability to recall and repeat his direction in sequence. The child enjoys the game more if the teacher makes many mistakes! He then chooses another child to take a shape, and the game continues.

The children should be given many opportunities for giving directions, such as asking the others to find a partner, or to hold up their books for collection. Individual children could send others one by one to the playground as they are ready, or to call the children to the table for milk or juice. With encouragement, they will think of many ways to do this, by names, by the kinds of shoes or colors others are wearing, or even by hair styles.

Cooking experiences help the children realize the importance of following directions on the package. The teacher may capitalize on every occasion when following directions is important, such as in times of danger, in taking medicine, or during a fire drill. There are times when following directions mean the difference between life and death.

Children enjoy playing games such as Robot and Master when one child tells another to do something. If he does it correctly, they change places. There are many singing games based on following directions.

Play a game where a child mentions a food. Others have to smile if they like it, frown if they do not, fold arms if they don't know, cover face if they hate it.

Teachers could make a stand-up cardboard seal or a bear. A mouth can be cut and a box fixed behind the head so that paper fish fall into it at feeding time. Different directions can be written on each fish; e.g., clap your hands, scratch your nose, and turn around. If the direction is followed correctly, the child feeds the fish to the animal. It is worth the teacher's time to make such a device as it can be used in so many ways. Shapes, letters, colors, or numerals can be written on the fish instead of directions.

Rhyming

Rhyming emphasizes the most important elements of word-sound relationships and is a skill necessary for beginning reading. Say a list of rhyming words inserting one that does not rhyme and ask the children to listen for it. Pictures or other visual clues may be necessary at first. Supply all but the rhyming word. "The cat is on the (mat)," "The mouse is under the (house)." Draw the children's attention to rhyming words in songs and poetry. Many songs lend themselves to changes in rhyming words. The children love nonsense rhymes; they don't have to be real words. The important thing is that the child's ear becomes attuned to words which sound alike. Some teachers collect things which rhyme to keep in a shoe box (string, ring, book, hook, . . .). These are spread out on the rug and children try to find the ones which rhyme.

The teacher can initiate an interest in rhyming by using objects in the room, or things which the children are wearing. "What rhymes with bear?" pointing to hair. "What rhymes with rose?" pointing to nose. This also helps to enlarge the children's vocabulary and increases awareness of body parts.

Play a guessing game. Show the children pictures. Say "I'm thinking of a picture of something that rhymes with boat." Let a child guess which picture it is. When he finds the picture of a coat, let him choose the next child.

Use the following:

Tell me a word which rhymes with blue. (Children say words, do, shoe, flew . . .)

That's true.

Tell me a word which rhymes with line. (Mine, shine, wine . . .)

That's fine.

Tell me a word that rhymes with white. (Night, light, height, sight . . .)

That's right.

Tell me a word that rhymes with hood. (Could, should, wood, stood . . .)

That's good.

Tell me a word that rhymes with brick. (Stick, sick, lick . . .)

That's quick.

Or this:

I like to think of things that rhyme like climb and . . . and knee and . . .

(Teacher continues to add words for which children provide rhymes)

I like to think of things that rhyme, like plop and . . . . When I get started I can hardly stop.

Use the commercial flannelboard rhyming pictures and

"Fun with Rhymes Activity Kit No. 1011, Instructo Corp., Paoli,

Penn., 19301.

Cognitive Thinking

Cognitive thinking is a signifi-
cant aspect and byproduct of language.
The clarification of ideas and the ability
to contrast, distinguish, and generalize
are closely related to language growth.
Children can be helped to understand
simple cause and effect relationships;
to make inferences; to categorize on
the basis of a simple criterion; to understand spatial relationships and polarities;
to make comparisons and to recognize the parts which make up the
whole.

Some of the ways in which these goals may be realized are
listed hereunder:

> Reasoning
>
> Generalizing
>
> Categorizing
>
> Describing and Comparing
>
> Spatial Relationships
>
> Opposites
>
> Identifying Parts
>
> Riddles

Reasoning

Ask the children, "Why do people have to earn money?" or "Why do some people need cars?" Discuss the answers. Let the children ask the questions. Involve those who are not able to verbalize sufficiently by asking questions such as, "Why do we enjoy looking at Mary?" Try to fool the children sometimes by asking a ridiculous question such as "Why do cats have puppies?" to encourage them to challenge certain statements they consider wrong. Ask them to explain why the question is wrong and how they could prove they were right.

Play the "I don't know" game. Show a picture of two apples. Say, "Which is the juicy one?" When children decide, tell them they are guessing, they just don't know. Play this game periodically so that children don't lose sight of the fact that there are times when they should tell a teacher that they just don't know.

After reading a story, help the children to identify cause and effect and to decide whether the story was real or imaginary and why. Ask children what would be a good title for the book.

Pictures which have been cut out and superimposed on different backgrounds can be examined by the children. A picture of a chef on a baseball field, or of someone wearing a swimsuit on a rainy city street will call the children's reasoning ability into play. The teacher should present such a picture to the children saying, "Tell me about it," rather than giving them the idea that something is wrong.

Have an "I wonder" corner in the room where unfamiliar objects and ambiguous pictures are displayed. After leaving them there for a while for the children to examine, ask the children what they think about them before discussion. Change the items every week.

The development of curiosity and reasoning ability is important for those children whose impulsivity may be high and whose behavior can be thoughtless. Many are accustomed to authoritarian or laissez-faire behavior on the part of adults, who seldom verbalize about such things to the children.

Generalizing

Generalizing is one of the highest forms of thinking. The teacher should take every opportunity to pull the children's learnings together by making and encouraging generalizations. Ask questions such as, "What can you tell me that is true of all dogs?" "What did you learn from the film that is true of all fish?" "Is this a picture of a fish or a bird? Why do you think so?" "How are a cat and a dog the same? Different?" "What is true of all elephants? Giraffes? Tigers?" "What is true of all these animals?"

By examining several items, encourage children to decide what property they have in common. After the children have learned to identify shapes and can distinguish between those made out of paper, present them with a ring, a balloon and an orange and let them consider what they might have in common. As they become adept at this, increase the complexity until they can understand the relationship between half an apple, half a glass of water, and half a cracker. Play What's my rule? Choose a number of children who have one thing in common, such as long sleeves, braided hair, or tennis shoes and ask other children to discover the identical feature. Encourage children to do the choosing on this basis.

Categorizing

Name some animals and insert a name of a child or a bird. As children detect the mistake, help them to say what is wrong.

Teach the specific name after the category. Show pictures of three kinds of transportation. "These are vehicles. This vehicle is a car. This vehicle is a truck and this vehicle is a bicycle." Introduce children to the group characteristic. If it's food, "Can you eat it?" If it's a vehicle, "Does it take you places?" If it's a toy, "Do you play with it?" The mathematical concept of sets may be used with subdivisions. "These are children, here is a set of boys and here is a set of girls." Explain as the question arises, that some things can be in more than one category. A carrot is a plant and it is also a food. Using a timer with a bell, give the children a few minutes to think of as many things within a category as possible before the bell rings. Do this as a group experience.

Make scrapbooks of various categories of pictures. If possible, find more than one picture of each kind. Print the same label on each. Seeing several kinds of dogs or trucks will broaden concepts. Let this be an ongoing project, about which the children periodically tell the class. Catalogs and trading stamp books are a good source for pictures. Make books about shapes, colors, vehicles, pets, and anything in which children are interested.

One child says to the others, "Think of a toy," and the others respond by saying, "A doll is a toy, a ball is a toy." Use many categories.

A game the older children enjoy is called "Shopping." "It" pretends to shop with an imaginary bag and walks around the circle of seated children giving each child the name of a food. They follow pretending to be in his bag. When "It" runs out of names, he says, "Bang." The bag breaks and the children run back to their chairs. The child without a chair is the new "It." Play this game using other groupings such as clothing, furniture, toys, fruit.

A variation of this game calls for two rows of children sitting facing each other. The teacher gives one child on each line the name of a fruit or vegetable. "It" sits in the middle. When the teacher calls "Oranges" the two children try to change places and "It" tries to get into one of their places.

Select three objects, two of which are in the same category, and call on a child to find the one which doesn't belong.

Play a guessing game where the teacher describes an object typical of a category while the children try to guess what it is. "I'm thinking of something that grows which is sometimes cooked and eaten with meat."

Read a list of items in a category and insert one which is different. For example: hamburgers, meatballs, hot dogs, apple pie. Children select the one which doesn't belong.

Children supply the missing word:

The car is also a vehicle. An apple is also a fruit.

A hammer is also a tool. A carrot is also a vegetable.

Use classification set for flannelboard.

Describing and comparing

Say to the children, "Tell me everything you can about an apple." Encourage them to include details about appearance, origin, uses, taste, touch, smell.

Provide many pictures and ask the children to describe what they see. The teacher can display several pictures and describe one for the children to guess. The children can do this too. Show a picture and make a deliberate mistake so that children can correct it. Let children do this as they are able. The children can describe each other in games such as the Policeman and the Lost Child, in which the "mother" tells the policeman what her "child" looks like and he identifies him by her description. A dime store badge helps this game along.

Help children develop descriptive ability by suggesting a

framework, "As soft as . . ., as pretty as . . ., as hard as . . .," Match pictures, pairs, colors, sizes, abstract forms, blocks, heights of children. Children can paste a magazine picture and the teacher can write, This is a . . .. It is . . ., using child's description.

Provide a number of objects or pictures of objects, which are needed on a trip. Have an old suitcase on hand. If a child describes the object so that the other children guess what it is, it goes in the suitcase.

Compare objects and pictures by size, shape, texture, color, and function. Use blocks, flowers, leaves, rocks, fabrics, buttons, grains, legumes, shells, tools, encourage the children to contribute to collections. Note large and small differences in similar objects and large and small differences in a series of objects.

Put a number of things on the rug and while the children are hiding their eyes, change the order or remove an object. Let them guess and verbalize on what has changed. Play this game with the children themselves. While they are hiding their eyes, change something about one child, push up a sleeve, undo a button, or a shoe, and let the children guess what has changed.

Put an object in a drawstring bag and ask a child to feel and describe it for others to guess.

Have four or five children stand in a row. Let class look at them. Re-arrange them while class has closed eyes, and then have a child place them in original order.

On a rainy day let one child hide under an open umbrella while another who has left the room returns to decide who is missing.

Ask a child to tell others one thing he can do with an object. Children guess what it is. "I can bounce it." It is a ball."

Child arranges three or four blocks or beads into a design and says, "Match my blocks." Chosen child makes duplicate of first child's design. This game can be played in small groups.

Children can use a teacher-made set of cards for finding likenesses and differences. Working from the simple to the complex, the first set of cards may be made with the different one being a second color, e.g., two blue lines and one red. The difference could be in position as three vertical lines and one slanted line, or it could be in the number of lines in each group.

Set aside a box in which to put things that are used together. Encourage children to contribute to this box. Children decide which things belong together, needle and thread, bat and ball, hammer and nail, knife and fork, can and can opener, brush and comb, cup and saucer.

A visual discrimination game something like dominoes can be made from 3"x5" file cards and an assortment of gummed seals, two of each kind. Stick two different ones on either end of each card; twelve cards would be enough. Children play this game in pairs or alone by matching the cards end to end. Seasonal seals can be used at appropriate times of the year.

Another game can be made by gluing squares and triangles on a piece of tagboard with a length of yarn attached in the center for an indicator. Children match the number of squares to the same number of triangles by manipulating the yarn.

Iron or press one leaf between waxed paper from each tree or shrub in the playground. Let children have a treasure hunt, trying to find the leaf to match the one in their hands. Make a feely strip of heavy cardboard or pegboard covered with pieces of material and different textures; sandpaper, ribbon, satin, fur, steel wool, cotton, velvet . . .. Children can take turns describing each one.

Another game which is easy to make is called Mailman. Using a commercial or homemade mail box, the children describe and mail appropriate letters. These are made of tag cut in small rectangles with stamps representing different categories: fruit, toys, birds, animals, fish. . . . They can be charity stamps such as Easter Seals, gummed commercial stamps, or the teacher's drawings. These can be placed face up on a table and the child "mails" whichever one is described by the teacher or another child. When all the letters have been mailed, they can be sorted into categories.

Spatial relationships

Children often have difficulty in understanding positional

concepts. Many children understand the concept but have not generalized yet. As a first experience, give each child in a small group a block. Say, "Put it over your head, under, in front . . .." Watch for children who are visually imitating. For those who are competent, provide pictures of similar activities, increasing abstract nature as children succeed. As a final technique, show a picture and ask, "What is over his head?" Find things in the classroom that are behind or in front of something. Flowers may be in a vase, blocks out of the cabinet. Use magazines for cutting and pasting pictures in certain positions. Make large background papers for each concept so that children can select appropriate one. The owl may be on the branch, the cat under the table, the car in the garage.

Give each child an envelope containing paper shapes which can be taken out and placed on the rug. Instruct the children to find the circle and put it in the envelope, on it, beside it, under it, at the top and in the middle, at the bottom and beneath. Put the circle between the square and the triangle. Which two shapes are farthest apart? As children become adept at this, let them take turns in deciding where the shapes should go. Introduce more complicated variations of the game. Ask the children to find a circle and a square, put the circle in the envelope and the square under it. Let the children experiment with the shapes to make animals or birds and comment on the positional placement. Use miniature farm or zoo animals and plastic fruit baskets

36

in the same way as the shapes and envelopes.

Draw shapes on the chalkboard and ask a child to put a cookie in the circle. If he is correct, he may erase it (eat it), and put another cookie in another position for another child to "eat."

Act out or mime Nursery rhymes which include positional concepts, such as the spider who sat down beside Little Miss Muffet; Humpty Dumpty who sat on the wall; the cow who jumped over the moon; Little Bo-Peep's sheep who came home wagging their tails behind them; and the little girl who had a little curl right in the middle of her forehead. The soldiers in the Grand Old Duke of York were sometimes up, sometimes half way up, and sometimes down the hill. The pussy cat frightened a little mouse under the Queen's chair. Little Jack Horner put in his thumb and pulled out a plum.

Play a rhythmic tune for the children to clap their hands above their heads, behind their backs, under their knees, in front of their noses, between their legs. Play Looby Loo.

Let a child hide a small object while another closes his eyes. The remainder of the children clap loudly if the seeker is near, softly if he is moving away from the object. If the child can identify its position when he finds it, he hides it next.

Cut three holes in a shoe box and cover each with red, yellow, or green tissue paper inside the box. One child holds a flashlight as he stands in front of the class, and turns it on to one of the "lights." Other children standing in a row facing him advance towards the finish line on green, wait on yellow, and stop on red. First child across the finish line has the next turn with flashlight. Discuss position of lights with children.

Capitalize on the occasions when children are sitting together by using positional concepts such as next to, behind, in front of, first, last, between. When walking anywhere with the class, ask the children if they are turning left or right.

Many fingerplays and songs lend themselves to a certain number of children standing in front of the class as Five Little Pumpkins, or Three Little Kittens, when position may be incidentally mentioned.

Plan physical education experiences in which the children verbalize about what they are doing, jumping across the rope, going up and down the slide, through the hoop, and running around the circle.

Children can learn left and right by having the teacher put nail polish on one finger on the right hand or a pipe cleaner ring. As children recognize left and right with parts of their bodies, provide them with the abstract concept and ask them whether the tree in their picture is on the left or the right of the house. Put a mark of some sort on the top left hand side of their art work so that they always know where to print their names. A song about left and right is included in the section entitled Musical Improvisation.

In the following poem, the children point up or down according to the words.

UP go the fireworks into the sky.
DOWN goes your mouth when you start to cry.
UP goes your temperature when you're sick.
DOWN goes the plate for your dog to lick.
Here comes the firemen DOWN the pole.
UP peeps the bunny out of his hole.
The umbrellas go UP when it starts to rain.
The pill goes DOWN when you have a pain.
UP goes your kite on a windy day.
DOWN go the piano keys when you play.
UP goes the flag every morning at school.
DOWN goes your head when you dive in the pool.
UP flies the mother bird into her nest.
DOWN come your pants when you get undressed.
DOWN you snuggle into your bed.
Pull the covers around your head
Until it is time to get UP.

Opposites

Read Provenson's book, "Karen's Opposites." Discuss it

afterwards. Bring out the fact that opposites involve a comparison.

Draw two lines. "Which of these lines is long? Which is not long?

What is another way of saying 'not long?' Short?" Give visual clues in

a pantomime game. The teacher says "hot," and shivers; says "tall,"

and indicates short with her hands. Other words easily acted out include:

awake, asleep, narrow, wide, happy, sad, low, high, under, over,

down, up, in, out, hot, cold, fast, slow . . . .

The opposite of up is down.
The opposite of smile is frown.
The opposite of fast is slow.
The opposite of stop is go.
The opposite of hot is cold.
The opposite of new is old.

The opposite of black is white.
The opposite of day is night.
The opposite of thick is thin.
The opposite of out is in.
The opposite of wet is dry.
The opposite of low is high.
The opposite of do is don't.
The opposite of will is won't.
The opposite of borrow is lend.
The opposite of beginning is end.

Use pieces of Opposites puzzle to teach concepts. Place them face downwards in random order. Children take turns turning them face upwards and making pairs. Use flannelboard reading readiness materials sold commercially involving opposites.

Identifying parts

Make a game out of guessing parts. Introduce one of the children to the class. "This is Betty." Hold a finger. "This is part of Betty. Now you play. This is a dress. This is part of a dress" (touch collar). Continue the game with or without visual clues, using the objects in the room. Lead children to make complete statements.

Riddles

Children enjoy guessing and making up their own riddles. Teachers find them helpful in those odd minutes between other activities. Riddles reinforce rhyming skills and descriptive ability. Those the children make up will be simple. I have four legs and a trunk? What am I?

Children could illustrate or color the key words in the following:

40

Ask me a riddle and answer who dares.

You walk up and down me and I am the . . . (stairs).

Ask me a riddle and say if you can,

1.   I'm sometimes a father and I am a . . . (man).

2.   I'm used on the gas stove and I am a . . . (pan).

3.   I'm useful on hot days and I am a . . . (fan).

Older children could write in the missing words, and all could sing to the A.B.C. tune. Pictures of the missing words could be held up for the children to see and they could choose the one which rhymes.

Other riddles along similar lines:

I'll ask you a riddle, and let's see who knows,
You've got ten on your feet.
I am your . . . (toes).

I'll ask you a riddle and let's see who knows.
I'm a beautiful flower.
I am a . . . (rose).

I'll ask you a riddle. Let's have some fun.
I shine in the sky.
I am the . . . (sun).

I'll ask you a riddle. Let's see who can tell.
I ring and I chime.
I am a . . . (bell).

I'll ask you a riddle. Let's see who can say.
All horses can eat me.
I am some . . . (hay).

I'll ask you a riddle. Let's see who can say.
I come after April.
And my name is . . . (May).

I'll ask you a riddle.   Who will reply?
Aeroplanes fly in me.
I am the . . . (sky).

I'll ask you a riddle.   Tell me please do.
I go on your foot.
I am your . . . (shoe).

I'll ask you a riddle.   Tell me please do.
I come after one and before three.
I'm . . . (two).

Use song, "The Riddle," on p. 16 in Music for Early

Childhood, California State Series.

Commercial materials for use with
subheadings in this chapter

Classification, opposites, and sequence.   Tapes and work-

sheets for duplication.

Rhyming pictures for pegboard.

Classification and opposite pictures for pegboard.   Ideal School

Supply Company, Oaklwan, Illinois.

Positions in space.   Set of pictures and worksheets for

duplication.   F. A. Owen Publishing Co., Danville, N. Y.   14437.

Opposites.   Help Yourself Frame Tray Puzzle, No. 4416.

Western Publishing Co., Inc., Racine, Wisconsin.

Bennett Cerf's Book of Riddles.   Illustrated by Roy McKie.

N. Y. Random House, Inc., Beginner Books, 1960.

Drama

Dramatic play

Dramatic play is another
activity that provides an opportunity
for children to develop language
skills. Being free and unstructured,
children express themselves and
gradually improve their sentence
structure through practice. Dramatization in various forms allows
children to communicate through
characterization and gesture. The teacher helps children to dramatize
stories and poems; to identify with other people; to use body language to
express ideas; to interpret ideas through pantomime and to develop
sequential thinking in the enactment of stories.

> Dramatic play
>
> Creative dramatics
>
> Role playing
>
> Pantomime

Dramatic play is spontaneous. While this form of play is
essentially impulsive, there are a number of ways in which such play
can be guided to support intellectual learning and concept development.
It is important that children see themselves as potential adults once in a

while, and playhouse accessories should be provided for them to use. The setting should be changed frequently and props should be available for the children to use in a variety of ways.

As children demonstrate their ability to build safely with hollow blocks, they have a turn to wear a yellow construction worker's hat and be the boss, with the responsibility of hiring and firing their workers for the day in a reasonable way. The boss gives his builders one warning if they are not observing safety rules before they relinquish their jobs.

Some boys have little opportunity to identify with male roles and therefore particular attention should be given to supplying appropriate male props. The following kits can be labeled for the children to use:

Store: Cash register, sales slips, play money, paper sacks, and whatever is being sold-- toys, shoes . . .

Barber: Scissors made out of tag, cardboard tube, barber pole, magazines, old shaving brushes and toy razors, play money, white shirts . . .

Restaurant: Menus, writing pad and pencil, apron, dishes, food pictures pasted on paper plates, chef's hat, cash register, play money . . .

Office: Telephones and directory, carbon paper and ordinary paper, pencils, pads, stamp pads . . .

Show: "Tickets," microphone, play money . . .

Hospital: Mats used for resting, doctor's bag containing stethoscope, bandages, raisin pills, white shirts, nurses' caps . . . (These can be easily sewn from shirt cuffs.)

Post Office: Mailman's hat and pouch, stamps, envelopes, paper and string, scales, teacher-made mailbox.

Dramatic play can take place outdoors, too. Children enjoy being gardeners, using a toy gardening set, a wheelbarrow, and short lengths of hose. The letter can also be used for firemen; fire hats should also be available. Cartons of "water" paint, painters' hats, brushes, and a Wet Paint sign made by the children keep them occupied indefinitely. A gas pump made from a cardboard carton, an old pump, and a box of nuts and bolts has the same effect. After a cooking experience, the children can set up a lemonade stand and "sell" the lemonade they have made . . . the list is endless.

Creative dramatics

Creative dramatics refers to the enactment of stories with which the children are familiar. The story is discussed and the sequence of events recalled. Characters can be chosen by the teacher or by the class. It is a good idea to select the children who are most unlike the characters in the story; a noisy child to portray a shy one. The characters should be discussed and children asked to show how certain feelings could be portrayed. There are no lines to be memorized and no formal audience. Each part should be constructively evaluated. Using words in context gives children enough meaning clues so that they can use the words themselves. Through creative dramatics the children have the opportunity to express themselves as other people do. Some-times it is easier for children to act as somebody else than as themselves.

Role playing

Role playing refers to a structured situation in which children act out incidents which have meaning for them. It should be a springboard for discussion. It can be used whenever there is a need to discuss how to behave at certain times. A situation in which two children want the same tricycle provides the setting for a scene in which two children and a "teacher" solve the problem. It can apply to taking a message to the secretary, explaining a school project to a parent, entertaining a visitor, or the use of good manners at Halloween. The teacher should refrain from approving or disapproving of any part of the action to insure freedom of expression. Following the action should be a discussion of the scene in which children identify things they liked and moving on to the feelings about the characters. Children's actions are usually more spontaneous when they are concerned with how the character feels rather than with what he says. Role playing can follow the reading of an unfinished story, the children assuming the roles of the various characters, and finishing the story. It is a helpful technique to use when children are having trouble getting along. They are asked to show what happened, suggestions are elicited from the group as to different solutions which could have been used, and evaluated on their merit.

Children need to understand that everyone plays a number of different roles in life. Using block accessory people, or the children themselves, discuss the different roles each figure might play. The mother figure might also be a nurse, a baby-sitter, an aunt, a neighbor, a daughter. Each calls for different behavior. Have children try to think of a situation for each role.

A television set can be made from a cardboard carton, the screen from acetate. A knob can be attached for volume control. Drinking straw antennae can be inserted in the top. Under teacher guidance, children pretend they are acting on a show. If they speak too quietly, another child turns up the volume control. When the set is not being used in this way, it can serve as an accessory in the housekeeping area or used to display a child's picture.

Pantomime

Children lacking in verbal skills can be encouraged to express themselves through pantomime. The teacher can whisper the initial suggestion such as "bounce a ball," or "eat a banana" while others guess what is happening. If the children have ideas, let them whisper their plans before letting them start.

Attitude pantomimes can be suggested by the teacher. "I have a terrible headache." "My feet hurt." "A present for me?" "Give me some." "Yes/No." "I can't hear." "Stop." "Come." "Just right." "I dare not look." "And I mean it." "No good." "I want to speak." "I'm scared." "I'm hot/cold." "It's hot/cold." "Don't know." "Be quiet." "I'm the champ." "Shame on you." "Goodbye." "It smells delicious." "Look at that jet." "I'm tired." "You're crazy." "Too noisy."

Listening as a Language Skill

Listening is a learned receptive skill. It can best be taught in a classroom environment which is free from interruptions and distractions. The physical setting of the room and the seating arrangements of the children should all be considered.

If we are to teach listening as a language skill, we need to recognize various levels.

Passive: We hear and recognize sounds but we do not react.

Simple: We listen with little concentration and little effort to recall what is heard.

Attentive: We listen closely for details and to understand what is heard.

Analytical: We listen with real mental participation, examine, evaluate, and respond.

Creative: We listen to build on what is heard and to act.

Appreciative: We listen purely for pleasure.

Every listening situation has its own purpose which the children should clearly understand. Skillful teachers employ a wide variety of techniques to encourage children to listen with increased attention. Each listening experience should be simple and brief and involve the children in a response of some kind. Actual objects appropriate to the listening experience often help to motivate children to listen. If the teacher is going to read the story, "It's Mine," by Bonsall, a rubber duck and a paper flower will go a long way in heightening the children's interest. The effective teacher maintains a good listening atmosphere by her sensitivity to the children's reaction to the situation. A smile, a raised eyebrow, a reminding gesture bring back a child's wandering attention more effectively than words.

Listen to sounds of the environment on tapes or records. Good recordings are available of bird songs, traffic sounds, and other sound effects. Let the children help to make a tape recording of the sounds of the environment and later identify them.

The children can close their eyes and try to identify the sounds they hear, opening drawer, crushing or tearing paper, snap of the fingers, the click of a lock. Include the vocabulary: banging, whirring, squeaking, gurgling. . . . The children particularly enjoy this type of listening experience after hearing the stories by Margaret Wise Brown about the dog Muffin and all the noises he hears. After hearing a story about a family, send a "mother," a "father," and a "baby" behind a screen so that the other children can identify the big voice, the middle-sized voice, and the baby voice. The children could also use musical instruments in this way, trying to identify a triangle, a tambourine, and a bell from behind a screen.

Sing Hickory, Dickory Dock, letting one child make the clock strike with a piano note or a triangle. The others listen to find out how many times the clock struck and if correct, they make it strike the next time. Children also enjoy listening to find out how many times the ball bounced, or someone clapped their hands and learn to identify numerals in these ways.

Play the kitten game for auditory training. Teach the children this rhyme: "The kittens are playing and having some fun, but now one is hiding. Can you guess the right one?" Six "kittens" play around the room. One child is blindfolded; one kitten hides. When the poem ends, the blindfolded child asks "Who is hiding?" The kitten answers "I am." The first child must identify the voice and indicate the direction from which it comes.

An example of creative listening is to stop in the middle of a story and ask the children what they think will happen next. Read or compose one or two lines of poetry for the children to complete. Put several pictures up, tell a story and ask the children which one illustrates it.

The Listening-Viewing center has unlimited possibilities. Commercial films and filmstrips can be shown in the usual way, or without sound so the children have to decide what the story is about. They can be shown once with sound and then with the children taking turns talking about each frame. Children should be asked to watch for

specifics, perhaps as a motivation for acting out the story afterwards.
Stop the film or filmstrip just before it is finished sometimes so that
children can guess what will happen.

As a general rule, children should hear repeatedly what they
are expected to say. Their listening to a description of what they are
doing will reinforce the knowledge that words can symbolize an experience. If a child shows by his actions that he wants the teacher to see
his painting, he can be told, "You want me to come and look at your
picture?" followed by gentle promptings, "Tell me." This may seem
obvious but it is a response that is often overlooked by the busy teacher
whose mind is on the total group. Similarly, a child will learn faster
when he listens to and repeats verbal instructions for a task.

Listening games

Jack in the Box, Jack in his box, sits so still. Won't you
come out? Yes, I will. Call out a child's name who is the only
one who does not come out of his box. He's the broken jack in
the box.

Jack be nimble, Jack be quick, Jack jump over the candlestick. Use a block for the candlestick and substitute a child's
name for Jack. This should be done in quick succession so that
children have to listen very carefully for their names.

Bounce the Ball. Children take turns bouncing the ball,
while others count. First one right has the next turn.

How Many Claps? One child claps however many times he
wants while others count silently. The one who guesses right
has the next turn.

What's the Song? Teacher or child hums the first line or
two of a song, the child who recognizes it first finishes it.

Farm Story. Distribute pictures to children of farm animals. (Wooden animal block accessories can also serve this purpose.) Read or tell a story about a farm and when children hear the name of their animal they turn around.

Tell it Again. After hearing a story which is familiar to all the children, one starts to tell it, points to another who adds a little and so on.

Whose Name? Clap the number of syllables in a child's name, others guess whose name it could be. When they have guessed, everyone claps it. Group the children according to how many syllables in their names. Give directions such as "turn around" preceded by a clap, two claps, or three claps. The children whose names consist of only one syllable follow the direction preceded by only one clap, those whose names consist of two syllables follow the direction preceded by two claps and so forth. As an extension each group claps a different rhythm when the teacher or a child points in their direction. When they can clap their rhythm, children can use their feet and stamp it.

Johnny Jump-Up. Clap once for the boys to jump, twice for the girls, three times for everyone.

Shapes. Draw shapes on the chalkboard while children close their eyes. As each shape is drawn the teacher asks the children to identify it as a circle, triangle, square, or rectangle.

Drum Game. Beat drum evenly and rhythmically while children respond by moving to the beat in any way they like. When beat changes, children form tepees by leaning against partner's hands.

I See You. With children sitting in a circle, blindfold a child. Point to another who says, "I can see you but you can't see me." Blindfolded child has to guess who spoke. This game can be varied by the blindfolded child pointing to another and saying "Make a noise like a : . ." and then guessing.

Who Is It? Let a child sit with his back to the others. Point to another who says, "Good Morning Mary." or (Santa Claus, Easter Bunny, or whoever is applicable for the day--headbands or hats are fun to use with this activity.) Mary has to guess whose voice she hears. If correct, the children change places.

<u>Do As I Do</u>. Tap or clap an irregular sequence--tap, tap, rest--tap, tap, rest. Children imitate the sequence and develop their own.

<u>Can't You Guess?</u> Teacher: Children, children, what are you doing? Children: Can't you guess? Teacher: Are you listening, are you listening? Children: Yes, yes, yes. (Vary this by asking different questions when requiring children to listen. Are you watching? Are you thinking?)

<u>Stairsteps</u>. One child plays notes on the piano while others respond with their bodies--higher, lower, same.

<u>High and Low</u>. One child is allowed to play high or low notes on the piano. Other children stand up straight for high notes, squat for low notes. When child plays two notes at once, others raise both hands.

<u>Who Said It?</u> Four or five children stand before the class. Others close their eyes. Teacher nods to one child standing who says, "It's Wednesday to-day," or whatever is appropriate. Others guess who said it. When someone guesses, the child who spoke sits down.

Teacher can dismiss children to go out to recess or to go home by saying, "Children wearing (sneakers) may go"; "children who have one brother . . . a station wagon, brown eyes, a dog," in many different ways. Try saying, "Three legs or eleven fingers" to catch those not listening closely.

As children learn letters and sounds, vary this by saying, "Children whose names begin with D," or with the letter which comes after or before D, or those names which begin like dog.

Stories can be written about field trips or walks in the neighborhood, each child contributing his ideas. Children can dictate a story about a cooking experience they have had at school, including the recipe, to be mimeographed to take home.

A large envelope can be kept for children's stories in diary form relating to any activity in which they have engaged. These can be displayed on the bulletin board together with the objects they have made. A nearby table could be used for clay or carpentry projects. The child's photograph can be displayed with the product or a photograph of a project which had to be dismantled and put away. The teacher should encourage the children to use signs for their dramatic play such as Jane's Beauty Shop, or Hank's Hamburger Stand, which are written and prominently displayed. The teacher can find many opportunities to write words which have meaning for children. The addition of "Mary's Red Collage," not only adds dignity to a child's work but is also a means of interesting him in beginning reading.

Give children a phrase to make into a sentence. "A little girl was. . . . A puppy was sleeping in. . . ." Write these sentences down and use them for story beginnings. A good time to do this is at Christmas or Easter. "Christmas is a time when. . . ." Old birthday or Christmas cards can be used to illustrate the story, or the story can be about a card.

Commercial materials for use
with this section

Sights and Sounds in the City, in the House, at the Circus, at Christmas, on the Farm. Sound Filmstrips Code 405250. Mc-Graw-Hill Early Learning Materials, Paoli, Penn. 19301.

<u>Sounds I can Hear--House, Farm and Zoo, School, Neighborhood</u> <u>Records, Picture Cards.</u> Scott Foresman and Co., Palo Alto, Calif.

Creative Writing

Many situations arise in the
classroom that initiate creative writing. The teacher thus helps children
to develop an awareness that written
symbols express the spoken word.
There is often a story to be told about
an easel painting, which could be
typed by the teacher and attached.
Children sometimes enjoy making

their characters speak and having the teacher make bubbles over their

heads in which to write remarks. Comic strip pictures can be pasted

with children's own comments. Sometimes a poem can be found or

composed to go home with the picture. If a child wishes to paint a story

picture, the bottom part of the easel paper can be folded up to write on.

The "story" can be very simple; such as, See my house. If the child is

ready to write, he could copy the teacher's words, or he might like to

copy only the key word. The teacher could write the words in yellow

felt pen and the child could trace over them in crayon. A word of

warning about the use of felt pens. The teacher should make sure that the words do not go through to the other side of the paper. Children are easily confused by this mirror writing.

Discarded book covers from the library, or picture postcards, can be cut out and pasted with a story written by the teacher and dictated by the child.

Children can compose their own stories and titles which can be taped and later written down by the teacher. Individual stories can be easily made into small booklets. These can be laminated by a machine which is sometimes available to teachers. This process makes the booklets more durable for use by the children who will then have the delight of seeing their stories in tangible form. When the children indicate that they are ready and interested in writing themselves, they can be asked which words they would like best to read. These can be printed on small cards and filed. The teacher can watch out for a pattern in the child's collection and the child can make up a story using them. The child's own language should be used as far as possible. Children who have difficulties in making up stories can be given starters such as, "I found a pair of wings and. . . ." If a child is interested in transportation, ask him to think of a story about his favorite kind of car or truck.

Children who are able can have the responsibility of writing functional words such as numbers or weather words. A sign could be displayed, "Today the weather is. . . ." or "There are . . . children here today."

Children can dictate invitations and thank-you letters to mothers and to people in the community.

Literature

The importance of good literature for young children cannot be overemphasized. Stories and poetry enrich and give significance to the child's everyday experiences, broaden the mind and stimulate the imagination. Programs for young children should include:

> Stories
>
> Fingerplays
>
> Poetry
>
> Choral speech

Stories

Most programs include a story time but there is more to a story than reading from a book. Show a few of the pictures in a book before reading it and talk briefly about what the story might be about. On another occasion, stop the story before the end and have the children finish it. Have them decide what might have happened before the story began and what might happen afterwards. Tell or read a story occasion-ally without showing any pictures so that the children have to conjure up their own mental images. Show the pictures afterwards and discuss them.

Use stick puppets for story telling. The children's easel paintings or drawings of people and animals can sometimes be cut out and mounted on cardboard with pieces of dowelling attached at the back with masking tape. Individual or group stories can be made up using these puppets.

The teacher starts the children off by saying, "Once upon a time, there was a tiny little. . . . His name was . . . . He lived in a . . . with . . . . He had . . . legs and . . . hair and wore . . . . One day he heard a noise. . . He looked up and saw a. . . ." Continue according to children's ideas.

When the children have made up a number of these stories, the teacher can type them on ditto masters and copy the children's illustrations for duplicating. Each child can then decorate a cover and take home an illustrated book of class stories.

Some teachers are born story tellers and do not always use a book. Some people feel, however, that the author's own carefully chosen words have a compelling power that is often lacking when others tell the story.

Flannelboard stories are a great help with children who are

sometimes unable to perceive all the elements in book illustrations. A large flannelboard and individual flannelboards are enjoyed by the children who make up their own stories with felt scraps. A selection of circles, half-circles, rectangles, squares, and triangles lend themselves to any number of variations. Illustrations from discarded books can be backed with felt or flannel and also used by the children. They can be put up in mixed order for children to place in sequence before telling the story.

Stories can often be dramatized by a group of children using puppets, but there is also value in making the puppets available for individual use. Some children will prefer to make their puppet sing before they are ready to make it talk.

When children bring something to share from home which is of no particular interest to the other children, make up a group story about it. An empty cardboard box takes on a new interest when it is woven into a story about a child finding something exciting in it on the way to school.

Help children to summarize their stories by asking them to say in a few words what their story was about.

Read aloud sentences in which words are left out. Ask children to suggest words which might be suitable.

Have the children suggest ways to finish sentences. "My mother was going to take me to the movies but. . . ."

Help children to make inferences by reading a paragraph from which they draw conclusions. "When I was running, I fell down and hurt my leg. I showed the teacher who fixed it for me. I was at. . . . She gave me a . . . ."

Tell a story involving several children. Retell, leaving one out. Ask children to tell who was left out. Do the same only add a character.

Fingerplays

Fingerplays have been a part of children's literature for many years. As children participate in the actions, they may be guided to feel and think as the characters do. The coordination of hands, eyes, and ears is a prerequisite skill for writing. Listening skills are developed and children learn to follow directions. Concepts are learned and reinforced. Fingerplays can also help children to learn cardinal and ordinal numbers and right and left. They are invaluable to the teacher as they hold children's attention for quite long periods of time and can also be used to fill in odd moments during the day. Hearing their own names in fingerplays enhances children's self-concept and feelings of acceptance by the group.

There are many books available on fingerplays. The following is included here as an example of how children's names can be substituted for those in the original. Instead of a kitten hiding and coming for milk and saying, "Mew,"

"Bobby is hiding under a chair." (Hide one thumb in same hand.)
I looked and I looked for him everywhere (peer about).
Under the table, and under the bed (pretend to look).
I looked in the corner and then I said:
"Here, Bobby, I have some candy for you."
Bobby came running and said, "Thank you." (Thumb pops out and
    wiggles its thanks.)

An example of how fingerplays can be used for various

purposes is the following which can precede a discussion on human

relations: on the children's level.

Big people, little people (hold thumb and index finger apart
    horizontally, then close together).
Fat people skinny (same as above, only vertical).
Grumpy people, happy people (appropriate facial expressions).
People who are grinny.
Rushy people, slow people (walk finger of one hand up and down
    other arm as rhyme indicated).
Black people, white (indicate those in group).
People in the daytime, people in the night (hands folded under
    cheek).
Rich people, poor people,
Walking up and down,
People who are smiling, people with a frown (appropriate
    expression).
People, people, people, everywhere I see.
What kind of person do you want to be? (Point to children).

Poetry

Language is intensified by the imagery and rhythm of poetry.

It stimulates the imagination, increases observation, develops an

aesthetic appreciation and provides relaxation. If there are difficult

words in the poem, they should be explained before reading. Showing

a picture or an actual object related to the poem and letting the children

handle it before reading enhances their enjoyment. The children should be given an opportunity to react to the poem without hearing the teacher's interpretation. They can be led to understand that everyone does not necessarily enjoy the same poems but that they should think about why they don't. Children usually enjoy listening to poetry while they are resting. Reading poetry in the few minutes before it is time to go home is a fine way to end the day. A poetry file at school is a good way to capitalize on a current event such as a birthday, a rainy day, or a visit from a pet.

Dramatization of a poem and appropriate sound effects increase the meaning of poems for children. As with fingerplays, children's names can often be substituted for those in the poem.

The author has a large cardboard figure of a boy dressed in overalls, and his feet are attached to a block, making him free standing. On the other side is a girl dressed in a long dress. The children's clothes are sewn with many pockets into which are placed poems mounted on different colored construction paper. The children never seem to tire of getting a poem out of a pocket and hearing it read. Another way of making poems available is to put them in the tail of a large cardboard fish or in the pouch of a kangaroo.

Choral speech

One of the best ways to help children learn to enjoy poetry is through choral speech, in which all children may participate. Children should sometimes be encouraged to interpret the words with rhythmic movement while others are speaking the poem. Teachers who often read well-selected poetry will soon find the children saying the poem with her. Many children learn to enjoy poetry in this way without the pressure to memorize. Rhymes in the form of question and answer are frequently found in books for children: Pussy Cat, Pussy Cat, Where Have You Been? What are Little Boys Made of? and Billy Boy being some of the best loved. Many others can be found in Talking Time by L. B. Scott and J. J. Thompson. Speaking in unison gives the child a feeling of belonging and security and many educators feel it can be used as a means for alleviating emotional problems. The opportunity to participate with the group helps a child develop poise and self-confidence, making him better equipped for individual work.

Musical Improvisation

Some children are particularly responsive to music. Improvising the words of songs is often a way of drawing out the shy or withdrawn child, and it is fun for everyone. It is a good idea for the teacher to acquaint herself with a number of core songs which lend themselves to spontaneous improvisation relating to children's

everyday activities. It is not important that the child's words fit the rhythm of the song, indeed, it is more amusing when they obviously do not! Individual children gain a feeling of confidence as their contributions become a part of the class repertoire and the group, in turn, is enriched by individual contributions. There are many well known songs which can be used for improvising and those which are mentioned in the following pages are numbered according to their source. The books and records in which these can be found are listed at the end of this section.

Songs can be a therapeutic way of solving interpersonal problems. If a child is obviously upset, it sometimes distracts him if we sing, very dramatically. If You're Angry and You Know It, shake your fist (stamp your foot, count to ten . . .), or, to an antagonist, If You're Sorry and You Know It, shake your hands . . . instead of If You're Happy (3).

When the children are learning their addresses, the teacher can sing to the tune of Do You Know the Muffin Man? Do you know the little boy who lives on (Market) Street? The child who lives there can then tell about his house and the children sing: Joe lives in an apartment house. . . . This song is listed under What Do You Do? (3)

She'll Be Coming Round the Mountain (2) is fun when the children sing (Mary) will be comin' round the mountain (or visiting our school), and She'll be wearing her (raincoat), riding in a (school bus), eating a (banana), carrying a (tortoise), or whatever words the children suggest.

Mary Wore Her Red Dress (2) is a tune which can be used to sing about virtually anything. Children can also formulate questions and answers to the melody. Where'd you get your dress from? Got it from my sister. . . .

Toodala (2) is a marvelous song for improvisation and anything that is happening can be sung about. How Old Are You? (2) is fun on a birthday and for using the question and answer technique. What Shall We Do When We All Go Out? (2) is also a question and answer song with children supplying the words. Jimmy Rose He Went to Town (2) can change to Johnny Smith He Went to School. . . .

Children can supply the words for Helping Mother (1), telling about their responsibilities in the home. They can observe and sing about seasonal changes in It's Spring (1). Fun With Daddy (1) when they go fishing can be extended to going shopping with Mother, swimming with brother. . . . Children can think of their favorite grocery items and substitute them for those in The Grocery Store (1). They can go on a walk and note the different kinds of trucks they see and sing about them in Trucks (1). Instead of going to The Dairy (1) they can go to the Shoe Store and sing about what they see there. Other occupations can be substituted in If You Were a Farmer (1); other actions, in Who Will Come and Skip With Me? (1)

Let's Write Our Own Words (1) suggests treating children's songs for special occasions throughout the year.

Teachers who do not read music find songs easier to learn when they can hear them. Many songs suitable for improvisation have been recorded (3). These are listed hereunder with suggestions for improvisation:

Good Morning to You. Greeting or goodbye song using children's names.

Hello Everybody. Use any other words.

Getting Acquainted. Good for questions and answers; who has the circle? Johnny has the circle.

Riding on the Bus.
Let's Take a Little Trip.　　Other destinations, vehicles, and
Riding in my car.　　　　　actions may be substituted.
London Hill.

Rig a Jig Jig.
Stamping Land.
Let's Go Walking.　　　　　Other actions may be substituted.
Busy.

Jimmie Crack Corn.　　　　(Turn around) and I don't care . . . .

On the Farm.
Morning on the Farm.　　　Other occupations and animals.

Go Tell Aunt Rhodie.　　　Other relations, other statements, or Go Tell the builders the blocks must go away.

The children always enjoy making up the words to the Bedtime Song. It concerns a child who tries to delay the business of going to sleep by asking for different things. Before singing the song, the teacher engages the children in a discussion about how they feel at bedtime. What are some of the ways they try to stall? What do they do

66

to bring their mothers back once they are in bed? The teacher then tells them about a little boy who was tucked up in bed one night. His mother kissed him goodnight (make kissing sound), and closed the door (clap hands), walked into the living room (walk with fingers on knee), and turned on T. V. and sat down (appropriate actions). All was very quiet (pause). Then she heard (to the tune of Someone's in the kitchen with Dinah), "Bring me a drink of water, Bring me a drink of water, now, now. Bring me a drink of water, before I go to sleep." Children sing and clap. The story continues with requests for whatever the children suggest. (Come and open the window. Come and give me my teddy. Bring me another blanket.) The mother becomes more and more irritated as she fulfills these requests, with appropriate repetitive actions, until finally, when she goes in for the last one, instead of kissing the child, says very loudly and suddenly, "Go to Sleep"!

Left Right Song

Children show their left and right hands for the bear, blink their left and right eyes for the owl, place hands on hips moving their "wings" for the bird, and pretend to shake hands for the boy.

Make up more verses using other animals and their environment.

Left Right Song

Music by Lynne Mason

1. A bear came clomping thru the woods, thru the woods,
2. A little bird flew thru the trees, thru the trees,
3. A little owl sat on a branch, on a branch,
4. A little boy met little girl, little girl,

thru the woods. A bear came clomping thru the woods,
thru the trees. A little bird flew thru the trees,
on a branch. A little owl sat on a branch,
little girl. A little boy met little girl,

clomp, clomp, clomp. He was such a fun-ny sight, he
flap, flap, flap. He was such a fun-ny sight, he
blink, blink, blink. He was such a fun-ny sight, he
shake, shake, shake. He was NOT a fun-ny sight, he

thought his left paw was his right. A bear came clomping
thought his left wing was his right. A little bird flew
thought his left eye was his right. A little owl sat on a
KNEW his left hand from his right. A little boy met

thru the woods, clomp, clomp, clomp.
thru the trees, flap, flap, flap.
branch, blink, blink, blink.
little girl, shake, shake, shake.

68

CHAPTER III

CHECKLIST FOR EVALUATION OF SPEECH,

LANGUAGE, AND COGNITIVE THINKING

Name _____   Date _____

Date of birth _____

	Key below	1	2	3	Comments
Enunciates clearly					
Is intelligible					
Correct volume--not too loud or too soft consistently--(one sign of potential hearing difficulty)					
Normal quality (not hoarse or nasal)					
Adequate vocabulary					
Willingness to talk					
Appropriate verbal response					
Ability to follow directions					
Ability to repeat sentences					
Length of response					
Structure (word order). ("I a boy bad.")					
Use of pronouns					
Use of adjectives					
Use of questions (Who, what, where, why, how)					
Use of negatives (He wasn't home.")					
Use of adverbs					
Use of verbs					
Use of auxiliary verbs have to, be seen					
Initiates conversation with peers					
Initiates conversation with adults					
Contributes to discussions					
Waits for turn to talk					
Expresses feelings					
Solves problems verbally					

Key: 1. No problem.   2. Some difficulty.   3. Is unable to do.

	1	2	3	Comments
Names 3 ways in which information is obtained				
Understands simple cause and effect relationships (Why do we need to put toys away?)				
Makes inferences				
Recognizes common properties				
Rhymes				
Distinguishes between reality and fantasy				
Draws conclusions				
Gives reasons for opinions				
Categorizes				
Makes observations				
Finds facts that answer a question (How many chairs do we need?)				
Understands and uses positional concepts				
When given a word can supply opposite				
Can supply name for part of an object				

Pronounces these words correctly:

baby	jar	nose	sugar	yellow
cat	key	pencil	toy	zebra
dog	light	rope	valentine	chair
face	moon	soup	wolf	mother

Dramatic activities

Role-plays spontaneously in housekeeping
  area

Makes himself understood through
  pantomime

Uses language with puppets

Remembers sequence of stories
  to enact

Uses expressive language in
  enactment

Listening

Listens attentively

Listens and responds

Makes auditory discriminations
  (High/low, near/far, fast/slow)

Identifies common sounds in environment

	1	2	3	Comments
Creative writing				
Contributes to group stories				
Dictates story in connection with own work (clay, paint . . .)				
Provides titles for stories				
Puts words into the mouths of his characters				
Literature				
Enjoys stories and poems				
Participates in fingerplays				
Participates in choral speech				
Recognizes main idea in a story				
Recalls details in a story				

Key: 1. No problem. 2. Some difficulty. 3. Is unable to do.

Note: This comprehensive checklist can be used in part or in its entirety for parent conferences and/or referrals.

BIBLIOGRAPHY

Books for the Teacher

Applegate, Mauree. Helping Children Write. Scranton: International Textbook Company, 1954.

Cohen, Dorothy, and Virginia Stern. Observing and Recording the Behavior of Young Children. Edited by Alice Miel. New York: Teachers College Press, Teachers College, Columbia University, 1966.

Cole, Natalie Robinson. Children's Arts from Deep Down Inside. New York: The John Day Company, 1966.

Fitzgerald, Burdette. World Tales for Creative Dramatics. New Jersey: Prentice-Hall, Inc., 1962.

Hammond, Sarah Lou, et al. Good Schools for Young Children. Second edition. New York: The Macmillan Company, 1968.

Hartley, Ruth E., Lawrence K. Frank, and Robert M. Goldenson. Understanding Children's Play. New York: Columbia University Press, 1952.

Herrick, Virgil B., and Leland B. Jacobs. Children and the Language Arts. New Jersey: Prentice-Hall, Inc., 1955.

Hymes, James E. The Child Under Six. New Jersey: Prentice-Hall, Inc., 1963.

Ilg, Frances L., and Louise Bates Ames. School Readiness. New York: Harper and Row, Publishers, 1964.

Landreth, Catherine. Early Childhood, Behavior, and Learning. Second edition. New York: Alfred A. Knopf, Inc., 1967.

Leonard, Edith M., Dorothy D. Van Deman, and Lillian E. Miles. Basic Learning in the Language Arts. New Jersey: Scott Foresman and Company, 1965.

Lowenfeld, Viktor. Creative and Mental Growth. Third edition. New York: The Macmillan Company, 1957.

National Council of Teachers of English. Language Arts for To-day's Children. New York: Appleton-Century Crofts, Inc., 1954.

Robinson, Helen P., and Bernard Spodek. New Directions in the Kindergarten. New York: Teachers College Press, 1965.

Salot, Lorraine, and Jerome E. Leavitt. The Beginning Kindergarten Teacher. Minneapolis: Burgess Publishing Company, 1965.

Books Teachers Will Use with Children

Buck, Pearl. Welcome Child. Photographs by Alan D. Haas. New York: The John Day Company, 1963.
    The excellent photographs in this book could be used as springboards for discussion.

Crowninshield, Ethel. Stories that Sing. Boston: Boston Music Company, 1955.
    The illustrations in this book could have been made by preschool children. The stories inspire children to make up their own.

Ferris, Helen (comp.). Favorite Poems, Old and New. Illustrated by Leonard Weisgard. New York: Doubleday and Company, Inc., 1957.
    This anthology is composed of poems children of all ages have loved for many years.

Fisher, Aileen. Up the Windy Hill. New York: Abelard Press, 1953.
    This book presents many simple poems for young children.

Grayson, Marion F. Let's Do Fingerplays. Illustrated by Nancy Weyl. Washington, D.C.: Robert B. Luce, Inc., 1962.
    Here is a large collection of fingerplays which will entertain children.

Martin, Bill. _Up and Down the Escalator_. New York: Holt, Rinehart and Winston, Inc., 1970.
  This book explores many different positional concepts.

Merriam, Eve. _Catch a Little Rhyme_. Illustrated by Imero Gobbato. New York: Atheneum Publishers, 1966.
  This book is an excellent collection of poems for young children.

Milne, A. A. _When We Were Very Young_. New York: E. P. Dutton and Company, Inc., 1954.
  These well-loved poems have stood the test of time.

_____. _Now We Are Six_. London: Methuen and Company, Limited, 1951.

Scott, Louise Binder, and J. J. Thompson. _Talking Time_. Second edition. New York: McGraw-Hill Book Company, 1966.
  This book presents many good ideas for speech and language activities.

Smiley, Paula, and Alma Gilleo. _Teaching with Rhythmic Activities_. Illustrated by Helen Endres. Elgin: David C. Cook Publishing Company, 1966.
  This little book of action rhymes and songs is a helpful one for teachers.

Siks, Geraldine B. _Creative Dramatics, An Art for Children_. New York: Harper and Brothers, Publishers, 1958.

Trager, Helen G., and Marian Radke Yarrow. _They Learn What They Live_. New York: Harper and Brothers, Publishers, 1952.

Wagner, Joseph A., and Robert W. Smith. _Teacher's Guide to Story-Telling_. Dubuque: William Brown Company, Publishers, 1958.

Books for Children

Berkley, Ethel S. _Ups and Downs_. Illustrated by Kathleen Elgin. New York: William R. Scott, Inc., Publishers, 1951.
  Illustrations and text help children understand the positional concepts.

Bongiorno, Mary M., and Mable Gee. How Can I Find Out? Illustrated
    by Lucy and John Hawkinson. Chicago: Children's Press, 1963.
        A little boy finds out there are many ways to learn about ants.

Brown, Margaret Wise. Important Book. New York: Harper and Row,
    Publishers, 1949.
        Many questions are asked about what is important. This
book is useful as a springboard for discussion.

Browner, Richard. Look Again. Illustrated by Emma Landau. New
    York: Atheneum Publishers, 1962.
        The illustrations in this book are open to different interpre-
tations. Each page asks a question. What do you see?

Coatsworth, Elizabeth. The Children Come Running. New York:
    Golden Press, 1960.
        An anthology of children's stories and poems from many
lands.

Dawson, Rosemary, and Richard Dawson. A Walk in the City.
    New York: Viking Press, 1950.
        Simple rhymes and pictures describe sights and sounds of
city life as a small boy goes walking with his mother.

de Regniers, Beatrice Schenk. What Happens Next? Illustrated by
    Remo. New York: The Macmillan Company, 1959.
        The story of a hero who didn't want to wait until he grew up
to prove his bravery. As the story progresses, the author
repeatedly asks, What Happens Next?

_____. The Little Girl and Her Mother. New York: The Vanguard
    Press, Inc., 1963.
        Everything the mother does, the little girl wants to do too
but she discovers she can do things that her mother cannot do and
vice versa.

Dorritt, Susan. The Learning Book. Illustrated by Elizabeth Donald.
    New York: Abelard-Schuman, Limited, 1960.
        Children are always learning but they will be grateful to the
author for interrupting them so they can learn about learning itself.

Earle, Vana. The Busy Man and the Nighttime Noises. New York:
    Lothrop, Lee, and Shepard Company, Inc., 1954.
        This book identifies and illustrates all the noises an old man
hears at night.

Felt, Sue. Hello-Goodbye. New York: Doubleday and Company, Inc.,
  1960.
    Two little girls and their families have moved so often that
it seems as if they are saying goodbye as soon as they say hello.

Lexau, Joan M. Benjie. Illustrated by Don Bolognese. New York:
  The Dial Press, Inc., 1964.
    A black boy overcomes an emotional problem by doing the
impossible for someone he loves.

_____. I Should Have Stayed in Bed. Illustrated by Syd Hoff.
  New York: Harper and Row, Publishers, 1965.
    This is the story of a difficult day in the life of Sam.

Lionni, Leo. Little Blue and Little Yellow. New York: Ivan Obolensky,
  Inc., 1959.
    Simple abstract figures convey the universal idea of rejection
because one is different from the others.

Provenson, A., and M. Provenson. Karen's Opposites. New York:
  Golden Press, n.d.
    Amusing illustrations of a little girl performing opposite
actions.

Rand, Ann, and Paul Rand. I Know a Lot of Things. New York:
  Harcourt, Brace and World, Inc., 1956.
    Dramatic and child-like illustrations of some of the things
every child knows.

_____. Sparkle and Spin: A Book about Words. New York:
  Harcourt, Brace and World, Inc., 1957.
    An introduction to the wonder and fun of words through
pictures and text.

Randall, Blossom E. Fun for Chris. Illustrated by Eunice Young
  Smith. Chicago: Albert Whitman and Company, 1956.
    A delightful and simple story of why people have different
colored skins.

Rukeyser, Muriel. Come Back, Paul. New York: Harper and Row,
  Publishers, 1955.
    A common experience of children who become separated
from the adult who is with them.

Stover, Jo Ann. Why? Because. New York: David McKay Company,
     Inc., 1961.
          Provocative humorous picture story book that speaks to
     children in terms they understand.

_____. If Everybody Did. New York: David McKay Company, Inc.,
     1960.
          This book amusingly explores what might happen if every-
     body did what they would like to do.

Vance, Eleanor Graham. Jonathan. Illustrated by Albert John Pucci.
     New York: Follett Publishing Company, 1966.
          The world is full of wonder; John searched for someone
     to ask until he found the answer man.

Webber, Irma E. It Looks Like This: A Point of View. New York:
     William R. Scott, Inc., 1958.
          This story tells how things look from different vantage
     points.

Wright, Ethel Belle. Saturday Walk. Illustrated by Richard Rose.
     New York: William Scott, Inc., 1954.
          A small boy tells of the things in the neighborhood he sees
     when he and his father go on their Saturday walk.

Music Books

1.   McLaughlin, Roberta, and Lucille Wood. Sing a Song of Holidays
          and Seasons, Home Neighborhood and Community. New
          Jersey: Prentice-Hall, Inc., 1960. Recordings available
          from Bowmar Records, 4921 Santa Monica Boulevard,
          Los Angeles, California.

2.   Seeger, Ruth Crawford. American Folk Songs for Children.
          Illustrated by Barbara Cooney. New York: Doubleday and
          Co., Inc., 1948.

Phonograph Records

3.   Making Mine Your Own. Silver Burdett Co., General Learning
          Corp., Morristown, New Jersey, 1966.